THE TRUTH S
CUNI

CW00739801

WRITING

A POCKET HANDBOOK FOR THE NEXT GENERATION

by
Joshua Free

*Published in by the Mardukite Truth Seeker Press in 2012
in the Encyclopedia Magica / Anunnaki Archives serial.
An abridged portion of materials from Mardukite Liber-1
also released as "Secrets of Sumerian Language"*

© 2012, Joshua Free

A POCKET HANDBOOK SERIES FOR THE *NEXT GENERATION*

The *Mardukite Truth Seeker Press* was founded in 2008 to coorespond with the inception of the *Mardukite Research Organization* under the sponsorship of underground occult vanguard – *Joshua Free* – known as '*Merlyn Stone*' in the 1990's. Thousands of copies of his books already have reached up from the underground concerning various topics such as the 'Celtic Druids', 'Ancient Aliens Theory', 'Ceremonial Magic', 'Occultism' and 'Post-Modern Transhuman Evolution' and, of course, the 'Sumerians', 'Babylonians' and 'Anunnaki' (to name a *few*).

Since 2008, over 50 editions have appeared of the core 'Mardukite Core' spanning approximately a dozen different discourses, called *libros* (or *liber*, singular) specific to the Sumerian/Babylonian (Mesopotamian) Anunnaki research conducted by the 'Mardukites' from 2008 until 2012. In 2011, a post-modern division of the organization was formed: 'Systemology', which focuses on the 'next generation' evolutionary movements. Joshua Free was first known as 'Merlyn Stone' prior to the public founding of the 'Mardukites'. During this time, his popularity was earned not from work on the 'Necronomicon' or 'Babylonian' systems, but general 'ritual' and 'ceremonial' magic. Of the popularly revived systems in the 'New Age movement', his exponent background is in Druidism and Celtic Wicca. He is extensively published on all these topics.

Drawing from the author's extensive works in addition to updated commentary and notes, we are pleased to provide a concise pocket handbook series with the next evolution of *Truth Seekers* in mind – *that means* YOU!

TRUTH SEEKER POCKET HANDBOOK SERIES
(*partial list*)

THE ANUNNAKI ARCHIVES. . .

The Truth Seeker's Guide to ANU
The Truth Seeker's Guide to the ANUNNAKI
The Truth Seeker's Guide to BABYLON
The Truth Seeker's Guide to CHALDEAN ASTROLOGY
The Truth Seeker's Guide to CUNEIFORM WRITING
The Truth Seeker's Guide to ENKI
The Truth Seeker's Guide to ENLIL
The Truth Seeker's Guide to INANNA ISHTAR
The Truth Seeker's Guide to MARDUK
The Truth Seeker's Guide to the MARDUKITES
The Truth Seeker's Guide to NABU

THE ENCYCLOPEDIA MAGICA. . .

The Truth Seeker's Guide to ALCHEMY
The Truth Seeker's Guide to CANDLE MAGIC
The Truth Seeker's Guide to the DRUIDS
The Truth Seeker's Guide to ELVES & FAIRIES
The Truth Seeker's Guide to ENOCHIAN MAGIC
The Truth Seeker's Guide to EVOCATION OF SPIRITS
The Truth Seeker's Guide to HERB MAGIC
The Truth Seeker's Guide to INITIATIONS
The Truth Seeker's Guide to the KABBALAH
The Truth Seeker's Guide to METAPHYSICS
The Truth Seeker's Guide to OBJECT MAGIC
The Truth Seeker's Guide to RITUAL MAGIC
The Truth Seeker's Guide to WITCHCRAFT

**MARDUKITE
CHAMBERLAINS**

THE TRUTH SEEKER'S GUIDE TO
CUNEIFORM
WRITING

A POCKET HANDBOOK FOR THE
NEXT GENERATION

by
Joshua Free

A WALL OF BABYLON INSCRIBED WITH THE
CUNEIFORM WEDGE-WRITING STYLE

TABLE OF CONTENTS

**MARDUKITE
CHAMBERLAINS**

THE ORIGINS OF THE WRITTEN WORD

Much debate has been given to the subject of 'human origins'. In every ancient culture, some 'belief' exists concerning this. In today's Judeo-Christian paradigm, there is a strong dichotomy pre-sented, waging an imaginary war between 'creationism' and 'evolution-ism'; as if these two ideals are so mutually exclusive if examined in a 'higher' 'light'. But the purpose of the present vol-ume is not to settle *this* debate, for we have *no debate* when returning our awareness to the parad-igm of ancient Mesopotamia.

According to the *Sumerian* and *Babylonian*[1] *cuneiform* tablet records, a separate 'race' or 'higher mind' of (humanoid) being, called the *Anunnaki*[2] had a part in creating modern man and many of the systems we have come to take for granted as part of everyday life. Great dispute exists over the 'nature' and 'role' of the *Anunnaki* among academicians and scholars. Their abs-olute origins are not blatantly revealed, but it is imp-lied that they 'come from the stars'. In addition to the 'ancient astronaut' and 'ancient alien' theories that have come forth, others have suggested that they were 'time travelers' or possibly even descendents (survivo-rs) of a previous civilization on earth prior to the 'mod-ern age'. Sufficient archival information concerning the *Anunnaki* can be gleaned from other 'Mardukite'[3] works[4] and going deeply into the topic would sufficien-

---

1   We will differentiate the two forthcoming.
2   See also *The Truth Seeker's Guide to the Anunnaki*.
3   See also *The Truth Seeker's Guide to the Mardukites*.
4   Mardukite literary works include many other texts by

tly deter the writer from the current focus, given what is already available elsewhere. However, these beings do come into play when describing the purely *Mesopotamian* paradigm of viewing 'human origins'.

Practically all cultural 'mythologies' share a unique belief that seems to also be anthropologically evident: that humans were essentially 'engineered' separately from the naturalistic evolving life on the planet and given a knowledge that something 'outside of themselves' was directly responsible for this. The *cuneiform* tablets speak of this 'outside' and 'intervening' force as a group of beings called *Anunnaki*, though they are known by a myriad of other names as well, not to mention those apart from their own ranks that they employed.

While it might be simple for one of the modern mind to pass mythology off as 'fiction', the elements involved in Mesopotamian Mythology are extraordinarily paramount and unique. When we speak of *Sumerian Language* and *Sumerian Mythology*, we are dealing with the oldest modern culture, one that is responsible for the onset of human civilization as we know it, and the 'fathers' of the true 'literary tradition' as a means of cataloging time in history, politics and government, law and property, and all of the programming that comes with it.

Joshua Free including the bestselling underground Mardukite anthologies: *"Necronomicon Anunnaki Bible"* (Year-1), *"Gates of the Necronomicon"* (Year-2), *"Necronomicon Workbook" (or "Mesoopotamian Magic*) (Year-3) and *"History of the Necronomicon"* (Year-4), etc.

Bottom line: the *Sumerians* and *Babylonians* weren't "stupid." The 'mythologies' that their writing reflects are not of ignorant people unaware of the natures of 'natural phenomenon', such as other skeptical scholars have often put forth. The literature[5] that has been left behind in regards to the origins of humanity, the creation of civilization and the education of humans in the sciences, all suggests a very intellectual and spiritual culture with a high understanding from the beginning, though a limited vocabulary.

The idea that ancient Mesopotamia is the 'absolute origins' of hu-man life is not suggested anywhere on the *cuneiform* tablets. In fact, given so much of the attention that genomes, language and evolution has had concerning Africa, the Sumerian records actualy corroborate with this too. Mesopotamia was, at first, a 'land of the gods' and the human-workers restricted mostly to African mines, but in time, this among many things, changed.

Although an introduction to the culture, mythos and ideologies of the *Sumerians* and *Babylonians* can be best found in preceding Mardukite volumes,[6] those unfamil-

---

5 See especially the Year-1 anthology, "*Necronomicon Anunnaki Bible*" edited by Joshua Free.

6 Most highly recommended are the "*Necronomicon Anunnaki Bible*" edited by Joshua Free, now in its Fifth Edition (now complete with the fragments drawn from *Liber-M* and *Liber-C*, along with the newly revised and expanded Second Edition of "*Sumerian Religion: Secrets of the Anunnaki & The Origins of Babylon*" (*Liber-50*) by Joshua Free, which now includes a critically relevant portion of the "*Babylonian Myth & Magic*" (*Liber-51*) materials. A Year-2 anthology titled "*Gates of the Necronomicon*" contains the text for "*Sumerian Religion*"

iar with this region and period of history in focus need not fret. Quite simply, we are dealing with the 'Middle East', or what is more correctly known as the 'Ancient Near East'. This aspect of history is not related to any elements concerning the political and propagandist issues facing relations between the 'Middle East' and the 'Western World' today – though the fact remains that much of the area referred to as "Mesopotamia" is now, politically, present-day Iraq.

The most ancient writings we have on the planet do not dispute that other 'civilizations' and 'experiments' may have come and gone on the planet or that the establishment of 'civilization' proper actually began much earlier. However, the chronology of the *King-Lists* and the development of human civilization for 'modern man' is separated by a critical event – one which is found within the cosmological records of all ancient cultures – called the *Great Flood* or *Deluge*. The records directly imply that *Sumerian* civilization (as we know it today) really began much further in history (into prehistory), in antediluvian times, prior to the *Deluge*.[7] The *King-Lists* appear congruent with this time

---

(*Liber-50*), "*Babylonian Myth & Magic*" (*Liber-51*) and "*Necronomicon Revelations*" (*Liber-R*). The most recent completed cycle for Year-3 includes "*Magan Magic*" (*Liber-E*), "*Maqlu Magic*" (*Liber-M*) and "*Beyond the Ishtar Gate*" (*Liber-C*), or the all-in-one Year-3 anthology available as either "*Mesopotamian Magic*" or "*Necronomicon Workbook*" edited by Joshua Free & Khem Juergen.

7 "This controversial event consisted of both torrential storms and the rise of ground floor water in connection to the melting glaciers and ice at the end of the Pleistocene period (regarded by geologists as ending approximately 12,000

scale, however, the shifting sands of Mesopotamia provide few clues for us directly (hence the importance of the literary artifacts) since the ancient sites were often dismantled or found in ruins from earlier times and then later rebuilt or built-over by cultural successors.

Archaeologists can successfully confirm the identities of the *King Lists* until 3200 B.C. (ironically the traditional starting point for *Sumerian* and *Egyptian* societal systems). The tablet records continue into prehistory, giving the periods of reign by various kings for another 420,000+ years in the past.[8]

Given the prideful and, albeit, egotistically nature that humans have an affinity for, it seems curious that in the annals of all the ancient cultures, 'language', 'writing' and the 'arts of civilization' are all attributed as "divine," or otherwise, *god-given*. Whether from the distant "stars" or remaining from the distant "past" (or even the distant "future," depending on your own interpretation of the *Anunnaki*), this separate 'race' and 'class' of humanoid being was revered for the 'higher' knowledge and wisdom at their disposal, but first and foremost as coming from something 'separate' and 'apart' from the 'human race' proper. This separation in consciousness actually 'fragmented' the natures of '*gods*' versus '*men*' and installed a self-correcting program of "authority" – in the form of "kingship."

"*Sumerian* and *Egyptian* records are very clear about the nature of the being occupying the seat of kingship at

---

years before present (10,000 B.C.)." *Babylonian Myth & Magic* (*Liber-51*) by Joshua Free.

8 "*Babylonian Myth & Magic*" (*Liber-51*) by Joshua Free.

its start – *gods*. The original 'overseers' were considered *divine*, having come from the sky – from the stars – and bringing with them the critical knowlege and technologies that would cultivate humanity. Their reign, [or rather, the public representation of their reign in their name] was eventually replaced by *demigods* (or *hybrids*), considered part-*divine* and part-*human*, until finally being passed to the control of a specialized segment of humankind."[9]

The means by which the *Anunnaki* were able to colonize the workers and make them suitable servants for the '*gods*' required that they possess the ability of *language*. Of course, a worker could be 'shown' what to do, but the installation of language abilities (believed to occur in humans around 100,000 years ago) was critical for them to be 'programmed' in consciousness. The closer to godliness they could be made, the more responsibility they could be given – meaning that the more they could understand, the more they could be responsible for understanding. Naturally, the *gods* were careful not to give away 'too much' (or allow the range of human awareness to 'see' too much) so that they might retain the perceived 'separation' between 'god' and 'man'.

For whatever the modern truth seeker might take from the belief paradigm of the ancient Mesopotamians, it is

---

9 – Excerpted from "*Babylonian Myth & Magic*" (*Liber-51*); corresponding notes: "This is illustrated by the recorded length of reign on the *King-Lists*, first being tens of thousands of years (*gods*), then hundreds of years (*demigods*) and finally the more 'mortally realistic' periods (*men*). In contrast, Judeo-Christian scriptures reflect a similar concept in the subsequent lifespans of their own genealogies."

from this main tenet of thought that societal 'systems' for human civilization were able to be implemented, using a class-system, a cabal of 'those who know', kings, priests, laws, codes, property and economy – all of which was wholly dependent on the 'written word' to be installed into existence and encoded into human consciousness.

AN EXAMPLE OF CUNEIFORM
TABLET WRITING

SYSTEMS: BETWEEN HEAVEN & EARTH

As soon as we begin to actually 'date' the inception of systems, there is always some remote 'remains' or 'discovery' that leads the mind astray in its focus. That "humans" existed prior to the 'birth of the systems' is hardly an argument: they surely did. But, what they constituted as "life" and "reality" was wholly different prior to the creation of 'fragmented systems'.

Having served to do the work of the '*gods*' and with the environmental conditions in prehistoric times changing with the natural cycles of the planet and its shifts and phases, humans were mainly 'left to themselves' by the '*gods*' for the cataclysmic period that appears to have swept through the earth, or at the very least swept over the archetypal consciousness (or genetic memory), at one juncture, of the entire human race.

Thousands of years before the scriptures of Noah (and his Ark), *cuneiform* tablets reveal the same motif, with one of the *Anunnaki* figures, ENKI, who had previously been most directly responsible for the final upgrades of the human race and its receipt of the 'arts of civilization', saves the 'life' on the planet by instructing a *proto-Sumerian* in the creation of, essentially, an "Ark" for the same purpose as the familiar biblical story.[10] Being only one of the possible examples, biblical scholars and historians alike have begun to reexamine *Judeo-Christian* texts that would appear to be pre-Semitic

---

10 For the Mardukite released account of this cycle, see the "*Necronomicon Anunnaki Bible: The Babylonian Mardukite Tradition*" edited by Joshua Free.

(*Sumerian*) in origin. In fact, most of the surviving scriptural records and *cuneiform* tablets are written in the *Akkadian* (*Babylonian*) language, which came to replace *Sumerian* during the shift in power from the original "*Enlilite Sumerian*" paradigm to the "*Mardukite Babylonian*" one. *Akkadian* is also the first language in the 'Semitic' family,[11] and ultimately the origin of the *Hebrew* language used by the Jews. Other relevant languages direct-ly influenced by *Akkadian* include *Aramaic* and *Arabic*, both of which can also be considered 'Semitic'.

Prior to the "Babylonian" fragmentation of 'systems' (used for the development of 'societal' human civilizat-ion) the *Sumerian Language* was primarily used for pragmatic utilitarian purposes. There was (and is) no true *Sumerian* word for "religion," the daily acknowled-gment and incorporation of the *Anunnaki* pantheon was simply the 'way of life', with the '*ziggurat*' temple-shrines being central to not only the planning of the city 'physically', but also the general "reality" or "rea-lm" that a citizen could occupy. Under the "Old Ways", each of the deities had established their own 'city-state' "kingdom" under the "Enlilite World Order". The limited literary tradition in place and loosely structur-ed proto-systems all reflected this.

The names given to the varying occupants of Mesopot-amia during ancient times are all related to their 'lang-uage'. The political names for regions would also be altered to be most relevant. In the period prior to the

11 A reference to the 'language' itself and not related
   specifically to the 'ethnic race' and 'cultural' group
   considered "Semitic". This 'linguistic' (language) grouping
   can confuse some seekers that might come to the (wrong)
   conclusion that the *Akkadians* were *Jews*.

rise of Babylon, the realm of Mesopotamia was divided between two lands (much like Egypt originally): the southern part (*Sumer*) and the northern part (*Akkad*). Although the two coexisted in the region for a significant amount of time, and even shared the *cuneiform* writing 'style', they were separated by 'language' and 'tradition'.

The "*Sumerians*" proper, were those occupying the *Sumer* region during the pre-Babylonian era, speaking the *Sumerian* language and observing the writing and up-and-coming societal systems from this perspective. In contrast, those from the north were *Akkadians*. By the time of the *Age of Aries*[12] (sacred to MARDUK, the *Anunnaki* patron god of Babylon), the *Akkadians* had replaced the *Sumerian* language and archetypal Enlilite paradigm with the (more commonly known) *Babylonian* or *Mardukite* one.

Exercising the original 'system fragmentation' of "kingship,"[13] the Mardukites were able to usurp the primitively operating 'systems' already 'fragmented' in 'consciousness' for their own gain. The heavenly work for the '*gods*' (for which the human race had initially been reared to) being completed, the 'material realm' on

---

12 The Age of Aries, circa 2160 B.C., was an intended starting point of Marduk's cyclic reign on Earth among the *Anunnaki*. His birthright for this was removed when he chose for himself a human wife, *Sarpanit*, seven generations removed from *Adapa* (who was born directly from *Enki* mating with one of the upgraded humans, instilling an even more accelerated product of human life on the planet, with the intent of them being a ruling class of *divine* or *king* blood.

13 Kingship – essentially 'godhood' on earth.

earth was all that was left for human command. The driving purpose still remaining: to serve the "world order" of the 'gods' executed on earth by 'Divine Right'. All of this consciousness programming, again, being accomplished and 'installed' into existence by way of 'language' and 'writing'.

In combining the two lands (*Akkad* and *Sumer*) of Mesopotamia under a single leader (now called the "*lu-gal*" or "great man"), a "new world order" is able to be established under *Akkadian* reign, that shifts the religio-spiritual focus away from ENLIL being superior in the eyes of humanity, and transferring the 'Divine Right' specifically to MARDUK and also, respectfully, to his father ENKI.

The manner in which "spirituality", "tradition" and "literature" are handled is forever changed with the new paradigm. These facets of 'life' and 'society' now come to primarily serve as the civic means of securing the 'Divine Right' to "rule" on earth and providing systems whereby this 'truth' can (and will) be accepted by the population. The archetypal concept of "religion" is born, and with it, the 'scriptures', 'genealogies', 'histories' and 'literary evidence' that we would now come to take for granted from a "religious system" – but for its time, this was a completely revolutionary step in human development.[14]

---

14 Additional details concerning the transition between the ancient *Enlilite Sumerian* tradition (world-view) and the first-fold fragmentation of this wholeness into *Mardukite Babylonian* are found in the Mardukite classic: "*Sumerian Religion: Secrets of the Anunnaki & The Origins of Babylon*" (*Liber-50*) by Joshua Free, now revised and expanded in a Second Edition to include critical portions of

The same 'pyramid-scheme' by which humans had been separated (in consciousness) and 'wired' to serve the '*gods*' could now be duplicated – the 'System' already fractured into sub-systems, however primitive they were operated before Babylon, could now be further and further 'fragmented' into additional "systems."

Anunnaki control of the 'heavens' and 'aero-space' rested with the *god* ANU and his son ENLIL, respectively. The material world, however – being the realm most integrated (involved) with human life – became the domain of another son of ANU, named ENKI, whose name-title meant literally: "Lord (EN) of the Earth (KI)."[15] Although the majority of archaic Mesopotamia became classified as "Enlilite" territory, the systematic 'arts of civilization' originally emerge from ENKI's southern city of Eridu. It is from here that we find the origins of true 'modern' human civilization, born not out of innate necessity or survival, but through the conditioning of the 'human psyche' (or 'consciousness') with the integration of 'worldly systems'[16] usher-

---

its companion work, "*Babylonian Myth & Magic*" (*Liber-51*). A collection of Mardukite transliteration work can be found in the anthology, *Necronomicon Anunnaki Bible* edited by Joshua Free, recently released in its Fifth Edition, complete and restored for the first time with the missing tablet material from "*Maqlu Magic*" (*Liber-M*) and "*Beyond the Ishtar Gate*" (*Liber-C*), both by Joshua Free with translation assistance by Khem Juergen.

15 The same *Anunnaki* figure also bares the name-title: E-A-, the 'syllograms' for "house" and "water" implying "whose house is water" (possibly referring to ENKI's patron city, Eridu, nearest the Per-sian Gulf, or else translatable as the "Dweller in the Deep."

16 Paragraph based on excerpt from "*Babylonian Myth &*

ed in by the "pen" of scribes.

Historians rightly credit the *Sumerians* with many 'firsts' for modern human civilizations. The more pragmatic of these, for the surface realm of urban survival, being roads, irrigation, pasturing, the wheel and chariot, sailboats, taxes, courts, law, schools, and above many other things, the 'written word'. While this list includes many 'grand innovations' toward societal achievement, it is 'language' and the 'written word', not to mention its effect on how one views 'reality' and 'truth', that is the most critical for our focus. The remaining facets are all 'sub-systems' further established from a 'meta-system' that is already its own fragmentation. Chariots and boats become a *transportation system*. History and scholarship become an *educational system*. The laws, taxes and assemblies become a *government system*, and dare we not slight out the all-encompassing '*cuneiform writing system*'.

The monumental innovation of the 'written word' is not only the cornerstone in diverse human development, it is the reason we are left with so many 'tablet collections' available for the modern seeker to explore today – without which we would have very limited means to glean the essence of the Mesopotamian mysteries. For the simple reason that they were seen as without "value" by excavators and grave-robbers throughout human history, in preference to jewels, gems, and other artifacts, we have been given a fortunate chance in modern times to unearth and uncover the secrets of the ages that have been long-forgotten until relatively recently. Humans have, quite simply,

Magic" (*Liber-51*) by Joshua Free.

forgotten where they come from and how they arrived here today.

The esoteric student knows better, understanding that the *uncovering of our past will reveal the future* and that those who can truly understand and appreciate the secrets of the ages that have been hidden from contemporary view in the world of lights will be able to use this knowledge to empower themselves and take the personal responsibility necessary to achieve true 'worldly power', thereby earning the chance to gain mastery over the realm of forms – 'forms' that have been name-titled and known through *language*.

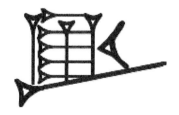

A PORTION OF THE AKKADIAN CUNEIFORM
"CODE OF KHAMMURABI" TABLET STELE

CUNEIFORM: WHEN PICTURES
EQUAL 1000 WORDS

Human history begins with writing. Academically, we consider everything prior to the inception of writing to be prehistoric. This means that the modern human experience has only been 'blessed' with this development for a relatively short time: 6,000 years at best.

Language, itself, is a predetermined set of communicative words, sounds, expressions, gestures, (etc.) that are all used to relay an intentional meaning from one source to another. Language is very different than 'writing'. Without even the use of 'writing' a spoken language can establish a shared meaning given to the many 'things' found in one's external environment in addition to the myriad of thoughts and 'feelings' experienced internally. Thus, language is a means of communicating personal experience using a means that is understood by a 'sender' and 'receiver'.

Given the discovery of tablets, clay coins and other artifacts, we can at least be sure that an established 'benchmark' or 'verbal standard' of language had to have been reached by the *Sumerians* by 3500 BC. It is during this proto-literate[17] period that one can begin to definitively find representations of the *Sumerian* oral language being solidified as proto-text in the form of pictures and symbols (even predating Egyptian hieroglyphs) called pictographic writing.[18]

---

17 *Proto-Literate* (*Proto-Text*) denotes a period *before written records*; literally "prehistory."

18 Also referred to as "pictograms" as well as early

Pictographic 'writing' has meaning in *any* language. Remember that there is a difference between the 'spoken language' and 'word sounds' that give speech meaning in comparison to that which is actually written down. The original version of *Sumreian* writing used literal representative 'pictures' to represent the various objects and 'basic' ideas relative to human existence at that time.

The 'pictographs' were also not dependent on a particular 'verbal language' for them to be understood. A picture of a "bird" meant "bird" regardless of what an individual's 'language' determined was their *vocalization* and *sounds* to mean "bird". The pictograms were originally based on what 'things' *appeared* to be, rather than the 'words' we might apply to define them. It is human 'experience' (or programming) via their 'native tongue', social exposure and personal experience that result in the internalization of the experience and 'language-based thought' when exposed to an external 'image', 'object' or 'idea'.

To the extent that modern humans have knowledge of at this juncture, the "oldest writings" of human civilization date to approximately 3200 BC. For the first time, written language extends past the simple and literal pictographs into more abstract symbols to represent the 'idea' of (and not simply the 'picture' of) something – to which we call "ideograms" (ideographic). Archaic *Sumerian cuneiform* 'ideographs' were derived from the original 'pictographs'. Note, that the proto-literate 'language' is not what changed. What the ancient *Sumerians* were developing was not simply 'language',

---

"ideograms" ("ideographic").

but the *very first* 'writing system' – *cuneiform* – a system that would continue to evolve for three millennium.

Archaic *cuneiform* writing replaces the early *Sumerian* pictograms with more 'abstract' or 'shorthand' symbols. The semantic mean-ing that would otherwise be appropriated to the 'realist' image becomes transferred by a less than 'picture-perfect' representation of the 'aspect' being 'named'.

For example, the original pre-*cuneiform* depiction (pictograph) of an "ox" looked very much like the head of an "ox" very literally. This image stood for the idea or concept of the "ox" regardless of the language being evoked into mind to interpret it. The original (Archaic *Sumerian*) *cuneiform* 'sign' for "ox" was the exact same image, but greatly simplified and without 'curved' lines of any kind. This same application was done to many 'pictograms' to update them for synchronous insertion into the *Sumerian cuneiform* 'writing system'.

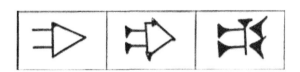

While the representation of the "ox" by a 'picture' seems almost certainly universal, *Sumerian* language took this a step further in using the 'idea' and easily 'labeled' *cuneiform* 'sign' for "ox" to also represent other related aspects – such as "cattle" as a whole. Another example: the word-sign for "mouth" could be used to indicate the "mouth" literally, but it could just as easily be applied to "eating" and "talking." The sign for "ear" might also be used to denote "listening," "hearing" and even "understanding."

FACTS ABOUT THE HISTORY OF CUNEIFORM

- The origins of the *cuneiform* signs are literal pictographs.
- The term *"cuneiform"* is *Latin* for 'wedged-shape.'
- *Cuneiform* is a "writing system," *not* a 'language'.
- *Cuneiform* contains *no* "letters", only 'signs'.
- *Cuneiform* is *not* an alphabet – its 'signs' *can* be used to represent different spoken languages, but the signs *are not* arranged by the *Sumerians* in a sequential phonemic (such as "A-B-C"). *Akkadians* later bring phonemics to *cuneiform*.
- *Sumerians* wrote *cuneiform* using the *Sumerian* language.
- *Babylo-Akkadians* wrote *cuneiform* using *Akkadian*.
- In "post-Sumerian Babylon," *Akkadian* replaces *Sumerian*.
- *Sumerian*-derived 'signs' and 'logographs' that retain their meaning in *Akkadian cuneiform* are called "Sumerograms."
- The word *"Sumerian"* is actually Akkadian from "Sumeru."

- As 'Roman letters' (seen in this book) can be used to relay any number of 'written languages', so too can the *cuneiform* script be used for various 'languages.'
- "Transliteration" is the transference of text from a *cuneiform* writing style to display it using 'Roman letters'. It still will appear in its original 'language'.
- "Translation" is the transference of meaning from a mess-age in one 'tongue' or 'language' and another. This can be accomplished with literary and non-literary methods.

Midway through the 3rd millennium BC, the *Akkadian*[19] influence swept through Mesopotamia and archaic *Sumerian* culture declined. In addition to preserving many of the customs, traditions and *Anunnaki* panth-eon ("religions"), the *Akkadians* began efforts to stand-ardize the *cuneiform* 'writing system'.

The first standardization of *cuneiform*, first and fore-most, was the 'character' or 'sign' *forms*, themselves. The introduction and wide use of the "scribe's pen" or 'reed-stylus'[20] allowed the formation of the writing to

---

19 Pre-Babylonian Mesopotamia is overcome by civil war which ended (according to "short chronol-ogy") with the founding of the *Akkadian Dynasty* in c. 2600 BC by "Sargon of Akkad" (also known as *Sharru-Kin*); not to be confused with a different (*Assyrian*) Babylonian king, "Sargon II", who reigns nearly 2000 years later during the "Neo-Babylonian" period.

20 *Stylus* – and '*style*' – originating from the Latin word for "stake" (meaning "pen").

be synchronous with itself. The myriad forms, sizes and shapes found within the ancient *Sumerian* methodology (rooted in prehistoric 'pictographs') fades away with *Akkadian*.

Cuneiform, as a 'writing system', was unarguably derived from the ancient *Sumerians*. Few elements of their actual 'language', however, were borrowed or adopted directly. The ancient language, referred to only as *"emegir"* [meaning: 'native tongue'], was too 'primitive' for the developments of civilization, and was replaced with *Akkadian*, though the 'writing' style remained.

Original *Sumerian* "root words," while spoken in *Akkadian*, came to be represented by similar 'signs' as their predecessors used. These "roots" could be connected to other 'words' to form elaborate compound meanings, and other "tenses" and "determinatives" were also affixed to to create a wide-ranging *lexicon*.[21]

For essentially 3000 years, the *cuneiform* 'style' of 'writing' became a standard 'systematized' relay of language (communication) in the ancient world, much like we find with later Greek and even with "Roman" letters today (a modernized 'literary system' that can also be conformed to apply to various languages).[22]

---

21 See also the original complete Mardukite "Liber-I" anthology, "*Secrets of Sumerian Religion*" of which the current pocket handbook is excerpting. A brief word-list is also included as 'Tablet-I' (from *Liber-9*) in the complete Year-1 Mardukite anthology, "*Necronomicon Anunnaki Bible*."

22 The familiar "Roman" letters employed for writing the *Latin* language are now able to represent the written language of more 'tongues' then <u>any</u> other 'writing system'. The *Latin* alphabet is adopted by the IPA (International

The later developing *Akkadian* phonetics[23] ('phono-grams') allowed for the evolution of *cuneiform* into 'syllabary'-styled writing. The new practices allowed 'literary expressions' for the way a word is 'visually' written (now beginning to emphasize how a word 'spoken' in language reflects in its depiction), provid-ing a 'form' or 'relationship' between 'sounds' and 'writing' such as is not originally found in the archaic 'pictographs' that reflected a more literal representat-ion of an idea (as opposed to 'abstract' symbols).

All of the rising 'dependent' "Systems" on the planet – those that contributed to create an 'elevated' worldly "social network" of the 'human animal' – wholly relied on fixed 'communication relay' in the form of stand-ardized 'language', or rather, the 'written word', to be effective. Writing, for all of its many functions or pur-poses, served to aid in the *Anunnaki*[24] "control" of the expon-entially growing 'human populations'.[25]

The establishment (or programming) of 'conscious-ness' (or psyche) for the growth of societal civilization

---

Phonetic Association) as a universally applicable "International Phonetic Alphabet" used to represent "phonetic notation" for written words in various global languages.

23 *Phonetics* – The emphasis on "sound" or "voice" of speech as opposed to the 'symbols' and 'signs'.

24 Even after the initial inception of *systems* by the *Anunnaki* specifically, the models and methods were extended to include those 'descendents' who exercised their own 'god-given' "Divine Right" to rule on Earth, in the name and image of the 'gods' who had previously reigned.

25 This paragraph based on *"Babylonian Myth & Magic"* (*Liber-51*) by Joshua Free.

as we know it today is, according to the ancient *Sumerian* and *Babylonian* tablets, a progressive combination of two ancient efforts: firstly, the birth of 'systems' in the Mesopotamian city of Eridu by ENKI (with the aid of his heir-son MARDUK)[26] and secondly, a complete ratification of the *cuneiform* 'writing system' by MARDUK's own heir-son, NABU,[27] who used it to enable the 'systems' as "active" in *Babylonia.*[28]

Resulting from the advent of 'advanced writing' and 'language', then 'societal' and 'civilized' "human psyche" became conditioned (or 'programmed') into shared 'world order' "semantics" to experience (and relay) "reality" by internally connecting context between two aspects: *pictures* and *words.* These two 'aspects' already shared a relationship in prehistoric and archaic forms of *Sumerian cuneiform,* but inefficiently for the growing needs.

The 'standardization' (use) of the '*stylus*' changed the nature and function of writing and human experience.

---

26 Appearing nowhere in pre-Babylonian (Sumerian) literature, MARDUK is the original "*High Priest of Enki*" in Eridu (the oldest 'systematized' city involving humans with *Anunnaki* after the 'Great Flood' (Deluge). Here, the *cuneiform* tablet records demonstrate an origin (birthplace) to the methodologies used in programming modern human existence, including: religion, magic, public records and other dependent 'societal systems' often 'taken for granted' by the human population.

27 See also *The Truth Seeker's Guide to Nabu*; otherwise see "*Of Babylon & Egypt*" which is 'Part One' of the complete *Liber-12* discourse titled "*Nabu Speaks!*"

28 Excerpted from "*Babylonian Myth & Magic*" (*Liber-51*) by Joshua Free.

The *'stylus'* sped up the 'rate' of which someone could 'inscribe' language into written "words with meaning." The new "pen," coupled with the methods used by the *Babylo-Akkadians* to write, effectively eliminated the 'curvature' of *cuneiform* 'signs' – something that is still found in archaic *Sumerian cuneiform*, linking the 'signs' back to their prehistoric origins as literal representative 'pictures'.

Rather than using the prehistoric models of literal 'pictographs' to represent things and ideas, the same meaning ('semantics') is employed in refined *cuneiform* systems using more efficient and wider applications of 'abstraction'. *Babylonians* adopted this new methodology of representing the 'concrete' with the 'abstract' – now able to relay an entire message with a few quick 'hashes', or more correctly, 'wedge-shaped' marks. With the literary system 'embedded' strongly in human consciousness, the mind (psyche) would develop a cohesive 'semantic singularity' between the asp-ects encountered in experience and the 'words' ('language') used to abstractly represent said aspects in 'writing'.

Academicians and scholars give into debate concerning 'language origins' and the 'birth of systems', it is important for the current reader-seeker to take into account the following basic premise:

"The solidification of abstract concepts and ideas being represented by words actually changed the way that the brain thinks, changing also the way in which one is capable of experiencing these aspects of 'reality' in the future. Likewise, the adoption of a 'label system' for fixed names, nouns and concepts creates an internal 'database' (called a 'schema'), which further manipulates memory and experience. The only real experimental abilities still at the disposal of a psychologist (or anthropologist) remain the perceptual comparisons able to be gleaned by modern humans of 'western' civilization' and those more 'aboriginal' existences. The general consensus is that these varied perceptions are 'evolutionary' advantages related to the environment one is reared to."[29]

The *Sumerian* language was wholly 'extinct', in place of the 'new' *Babylonian-Akkadian* paradigm by the Age of Aries (c. 2160 BC). By 2000 BC, *Babylonian* civil law required that all "transactions" be made 'real' by involving the 'realm'. They were all documented and duplicated – sometimes even *triplicated* – by an official class of 'priests',[30] called *"scribes."*

---

29 Excerpted from a footnote in *"Babylonian Myth & Magic"* (*Liber-51*) by Joshua Free.

30 Aside from the "King," "Queen" and 'royal' or 'dynastic' succession of presumably 'separate' blood than that of 'average' folk (sometimes called "Dragonblood" in esoterica), there were only a few other primary 'classes' of citizen in ancient Mesopotamia, though they could be further divided into 'sub-classes'. There were primarily 'commoners' and 'slaves'. The only other were 'officials' – those who played a key role in 'societal systems' from a time before 'church' and 'state' were ever frag-mented from each other the first time (something that the 'systems fracture' in *Babylon* allowed). To fully understand this archetypal model, it is suggested to review the *"Necronomicon Anunnaki Bible"* edited by Joshua Free, in addition to its corresponding work in the *"Gates of the Necronomicon"* anthology, including *"Sumerian Religion"* (*Liber-50*), *"Babylonian Myth & Magic* (*Liber-51*) and *Necronomicon Revelations* (*Liber-R*). Most recently, *"Sumerian Religion: Secrets of the Anunnaki & The Origins*

For an exceptionally extended period of human history, only the perceptibly 'highest' (or 'elite') classes of
citizen were required (or fluent) in the 'arts' of *reading*
and *writing*. As a result, a dependency on the scribe-
priests emerged, requiring the written word and its
representation to be 'interpreted' by a third-party for
it to have any meaning to the 'commoner'. Any discov-
ered indiscretions or falsehood relayed in this process
were severely punished. This was necessary to stren-
gthen faith (and preserve) the belief held by the population that the 'written word' (found on life-altering
'documents' regarding history, ownership and religion)[31] represented 'reality' "one-to-one."

A rise in 'official documentation' let to the 'signing' of
one's own name to 'verify' a piece of writing – particularly those pertaining to civil law, such as 'property' or
the exchange of goods. Before the inception of 'signet-
rings',[32] the 'cylinder seal' was invented – a clay-const-

---

 of Babylon" (*Liber-50*) has been revised and expanded to
 also include critical excerpts from "*Babylonian Myth &*
 Magic" (*Liber-51*).

31 A tradition eventually developed toward the construction
 and maintenance of *royal libraries*, also doubling (in
 Babylonia) as 'temple-shrines' to the *Anunnaki* 'god',
 NABU, heir-son of MARDUK. Efforts to create and
 preserve 'archival libraries' later occurred elsewhere in
 Mesopotamia, copied and inscribed (circulated) by a class
 of scribe-priest under the direction of the 'current' reigning
 "authority."

32 Made popular with the use of 'waxen seals' when the written
 word (documents) became 'paper-based' (no longer
 restricted to impressions or inscriptions made in stone and
 clay). Signet rings are essentially a personalized 'logograph' or 'insignia' meant to represent the 'author-ity' writing
 it.

ructed 'signature-seal' uniquely fashioned for an individual to be used as a means of 'signing' or 'validating' a piece of writing.[33]

'Cylinder seals' were worn or carried like a large "bead." This type of 'seal' is best compared to the means of 'documentation' that contemporary humans are systematically reliant on to prove one's own "identity" (to the extent that the 'state' or 'civil system' is concerned). The 'cylinders' were rolled across the tablet surface to add an indicative 'rectangular' stamp or impression.

The 'covert' governing 'body' of individuals that brought the inception of the societal 'systems' also regulated the means used to integrate 'written truth' into 'social consciousness'. Definitions, semantics, styles, sound use, the perceived limitations of 'knowledge' and 'reason', not to mention the boundaries of the 'realm', now set down to *remain* and be *understood* for future generations, completely changed the human range of experience of existence.

---

33 "The scribe-priests of NABU developed a unique way of enclosing and preserving a signed clay tablet (deterring possible attempts of tampering or alteration) within a clay envelope that bore a duplicated signed document-inscription on the outside – and in special circumstances of high importance a third copy would be retained by an archivist in addition to the individual 'parties' involved. This progression toward trust-in-writing led to the development of the first form of 'banking' and 'commerce' that could be notated with 'written receipts'. The 'official deed' allowed for civil law pertaining to 'personal property' and the establishment of a state-recognized system of 'real estate'." – from *"Babylonian Myth & Magic"* (*Liber-51*) by Joshua Free

LINGUISTIC ANALYSIS:
SYNTAX & SEMANTICS

"With the evolution of the *cuneiform* 'writing system' in history, the face of 'religion' changed into the more familiar 'versions' of Mesopotamian records that it is best defined by today – based on the *surviving writings* still at our disposal. In pre-Babylonian Sumer, the 'temple-shrine' *ziggurats* acted as the earth-home-bases for a respective *Anunnaki* 'deity' the building was dedicated to. The 'priests' served as intermediaries between the '*god*' and the human population."

~ Joshua Free
Babylonian Myth & Magic, (Liber-51)[34]

The standardized implementation of writing being established, the historical, mystical and religious tablets still surviving from *Sumerian* periods could now be recopied not only to solidify and protect the integrity of an original tradition, but actually make *manipulating* them possible – this occurred in *Babylonia* when 'mythology' was used to elevate MARDUK to supremacy, begin-ning officially at the turn of the Age of Aries (c. 2160 BC).

Being 'fragmented' once, the method for doing so left the way open to be further 'fragmented' by language and perception in the future, giving rise to a plethora of paradigms or 'interpretations' of 'reality' [meaning, experience in the realm] throughout the remainder of

---

34 Also reprinted as "*The Truth Seeker's Guide to Babylon.*"

human existence. This rudimentary civil logic encoding serves as the basis for most of the societal 'systems' still active today.

FACTS ABOUT EXISTENTIAL LINGUISTIC ENCODING

- *Reality* is based on 'personal experience' of the *Realm*.
- The *Realm* is, primarily, the 'World of Light' that we can 'see' (or 'experience') within the limited range of human sensory perception.
- The 'World of Light' is separated into *forms* that require coherent classification as *things* within a predetermined 'language-based system' in order to carry any semantic (or 'conceptual') *meaning* as part of a functioning 'program'.
- 'Data-collection' concerning the nature of *Reality* is the basic function/purpose of 'writing'.
- Internal 'interpretation' by consciousness equates what 'data' is collected as *facts*. [Thus, 'writing' (or, '*words that stay*'[35]) are *facts* collected about *Reality*.]
- Cohesive/coherent 'personal experience' is dependent on the 'syntax' and 'semantics' from a socially-derived language (and writing) system for interpretation and evaluation by an individual concerning *Reality*.
- *Cuneiform* script illustrates the oldest and original writings defining human *Reality* at the inception of civilization.

---

35 In the motion picture "*The Dark Crystal*," the concept of 'writing' is defined as "*words that stay.*"

- 'Historical' tablets describing successive eras of humanity the deeds of kings and heroes, and even 'Cosmological' tablets relaying prehistoric deeds of the '*gods*' become dictated to the population and presented as *fact*.
- From the human perspective – *words impart reality.*

The history of word origins, the development of words within 'writing systems' and their changing (or evolving) meanings (or semantics) through time all lay within the academic domain of *etymology*. Sadly, most scholarly explorations into words, writing and language seem to dismiss the revolutionary contributions provided by the ancient Mesopotamia, preferring to focus on the relatively more recent (and tangible) 'classical languages' – such as those from the late-Egyptians, Greeks and eventually Romans.

A lack of coherent data (and perhaps, ambition) have kept the secrets of *Sumerian* language apart from the traditional studies made into the origins and development of language. Attempts to resurrect and understand the 'systems' emerging from the ancient *Sumerians* and *Babylonians* have only begun within the last century and the majority of the work (and findings) has not been a centralized focus, by any means, to 'mainstream' populations; something that the modern Mardukite[36] movement consistently strive to change.

---

36 For further background see *The Truth Seeker's Guide to the Mardukites*; the special 'New Babylon Rising' issue *"Modern Mardukite 2012"* (also reprinted in the new full color deluxe edition *"Mardukite Magick: The Rites & Rituals of the Babylonian Anunnaki Tradition."*

In this present volume, we are introducing a unique and archetypal 'writing system' that is otherwise incredibly 'foreign' and 'esoteric' in itself, without even being presented under the veils of mystery, magic and mythology that typically accompanies these pursuits.[37] Sufficient years of research and literary publications (from the *Mardukites*) already provide this for those who seek it, but our current emphasis is strictly the 'writing system'.

As explained throughout this volume, the *cuneiform* style of writing is just that: a *style* – the *original* 'style', born from the use of a '*stylus*' in its forming. It is also not an alphabet, and in its originating archaic *Sumerian* form, is without 'phonetics'. Given that it has not been used by the surface world for essentially two millennium and the lack of well-founded accessible materials, the pursuit of understanding the *Sumerian* language, or *cuneiform* in general, becomes incredibly ominous and mysterious because of how 'removed' the concept (paradigm) is from 'today'.

---

37 Highly acclaimed supplemental volumes recommended for the reader-seeker include: "*Necronom-icon Anunnaki Bible*," the "*Gates of the Necronomicon*" anthology (which includes the text to "*Sumerian Religion*," "*Babylonian Myth & Magic*" and "*Necronomicon Revelations*"), in addition to two 'supplemental' companion "handbook" releases, "*Mardukite Guardians of the Gates*" and "*Mardukite Wizards of the Wastelands*", and finally the pocket companion, "*The Book of Marduk by Nabu*." A literary archive of other related works are also available from the Mardukites.

LOGOGRAMS
Pictographic, Ideographic, Syllabographic

Rather than a simple 'alphabet', organized consecut-ively (numeric) and based on the sounds found in the vocalization of the language in speech, the original *Sumerian* writings are made up of over 1,000 different 'pictures', usually called '*pictographs*'. These were later supplemented with '*ideographs*' to represent diverse meanings from a 'root' word, or extensions of the same, that were no longer limited to the 'literal' repre-sentation of the picture or simplified logographic symbol.

A *logograph*, in any of its forms, is usually the represe-ntation of a simple (single) 'word' or 'word-part'.[38] This is graphically represented by a symbol, or in the case of *cuneiform*, by a 'sign'. With the evolution of post-Sumerian *cuneiform* by the *Babylonians* and other later contributors, *logographic* writing developed into, what is called, *syllabographic* – the written forms began to represent the actual 'sounds' of a word, much like we use language today.

PHONETICS – Morphemes & Phonograms

According to the classifications offered in contempor-ary linguistic analysis, the *morpheme* is the "smallest 'unit' of language." This is generally meant to be more than, in the case of the modern Roman alphabet for the English language, a simple letter; for example, "B." By itself, the letter "B" is not truly semantically meaning-

---

38 '*word-parts*' – called "morphemes."

ful and therefore is not really a *morpheme.*

A *morpheme* is also not a simple 'syllable', which would be the "smallest 'unit' of spoken language syntax." Each of the syllables may become represented by their own 'signs', but that does not necessarily guarantee that they are earning greater 'meaning' in the context of language. A *morpheme* should be semantically meaningful, even if not as a freestanding proper word.

For example: "*un-*" and "*non-*" are both syllables; they both have semantic meaning by themselves (indicative of 'negation' in English); cannot be reduced to a 'smaller' "unit" of language or standalone as a "word" proper. Both are *morphemes* that can lend their own meaning and phonetic sound to other 'root' words. A single 'sign' generally only represents a 'root word' or applicable 'affixes' that can be added to intentionally modify the meaning.

SEMANTICS – Signs, Symbols & Syntax

About as popular among the up-and-coming next generational scholars of today as *etymology* has proven, the intellectual realm of *semantics* is a dedicated study to the meaning (denotation) of words and writing, the context of the words within its own language in addition to comparing the literal meaning, symbolic signs and vocalizations with other known languages. The way in which certain words are used together and the manner in which the language is predetermined to be coherent when used leads to the *syntax* or 'structure' that can be appropriately defined based on a given language. [For example, the concepts of a 'sentence', 'paragraph', 'exclamation', 'begging-the-question' (or other 'fallacies') are all relative to the individual 'context' of a language.]

As will become increasingly clear by examining the various transliterated[39] word-lists and *cuneiform* depictions in more intensive studies of *cuneiform* language use:[40]

- The same representative 'word-name' can be used for different conceptual 'meanings'.
- The same representative 'sign' can be used to denote different 'word-names'.
- The same 'meanings' can be represented by different 'word-names' and 'signs'.

Examining the main 'dictionary' sections of the current volume, the reader-seeker will notice that the entries are catalogued using a modern 'alphabetical ordering' that is based on the transliterated *Sumerian* root word in combination with the related (archaic) pictographic *cuneiform* sign from the Sumerian language.

---

39 *Transliteration* – to bring, for our purposes, the *logographic* depictions of the *cuneiform* styling into a more familiar 'paradigm' – for example, the "Roman" *Latin* alphabet. Words will still appear in their foreign (native) language, but will have been converted to 'standardized' letters, usually representative of the 'spoken' word-name, which lends significant aid to a piece's "translation."

40 See the complete anthology "*Secrets of Sumerian Language*" from which the current pocket handbook is excerpted from by exlcluding the main 'dictionary' portions. General word-lists can also be found as "Tablet-I" (from *Liber-9*) in the complete Year-1 anthology "*Necronomicon Anunnaki Bible*" edited by Joshua Free.

Given the rising interest and current emphasis being the *"Sumerian Language,"* it seemed only fitting by the current editor and supporting research staff to make the cryptic and antiquated *Sumerian* element of Meso-potamian language the main focus of this work.[41] The fact remains, however, that the main 'corpus' of mat-erials that are used in the "Mardukite" research (as well as more mainstream pursuits), including those[42] which are misappropriated by scholars and trend-seek-ers as '*Sumerian*' when they are not, come from *Babylon* and are found on tablets that depict a more refined *cuneiform* written with a post-*Sumerian* dialect, usually the *Akkadian* language.

In addition to the large graphic depiction of the *Sumer-ian cuneiform* 'sign', *Sumerian* 'word-name' and corres-ponding 'definition' or 'key words' to hundreds of basic

---

41 Noting the complete "Liber-I" treatise on the history and development of the cuneiform writing system as given in the 2012 release *"Secrets of Sumerian Language"* with an extensive introductory illustrated dictionary-lexicon, which originally began being compiled by the Mardukites in 2009 for internal purposes only but was later released to the public including the text excerpted for this pocket guide.

42 For example, the *"Enuma Elis"* or *"Epic of Creation,"* which is so notably referred to by contemp-oraries as "Sumerian" in origin, is actually a post-*Sumerian* treatise forged in *Babylon* by the priest-scribes of NABU, who developed the original religious fragmentation away from an 'Enlilite Sumerian' paradigm and toward the 'Mardukite' one that *Babylonia* became famous for. A large translation collection of such tablet work was consolidated into the original "Year-1" Mardukite anthology, *"Necronomicon Anunnaki Bible"* edited by Joshua Free, recently revised and expanded to include the tablet materials form the "Year-3" work, including the complete *"Maqlu"* text.

'roots', there is correlative in-formation (and supplemental 'word-lists') that demonstrate the immediate evolution of the *Sumerian* 'system' via the post-*Sumerian* "*Akkadian*" language (noted in the dictionary entries alongside the "Akk." designation).

The *Akkadian* word (or words) given with each entry have been selected primarily based on the 'semantic meaning' of the *Sumerian* 'sign' (given as the definition). The equivalency is based on the definition and not necessarily a direct 'evolution' of the original *Sumerian* 'sign' as a graphic representation.

When using *cuneiform*, the orientation of writing, regardless of the 'language' that the script-style is being used for, is always from 'left-to-right'. The 'compounding' words found in the language are often meant to be 'read' or 'interpreted' "backwards" since they are written in the order of an aspect's 'generalization': usually beginning with the main (primary) subject, followed by supporting (descriptive) words pertaining to the 'root'. Consider the 'breakdowns' of some common *Sumerian* compound words:

KAMAH *ka-mah*	KA (gate) + MAH (great) = "Great Gate" (city gate)
LUGAL *lu-gal*	LU (man) + GAL (big) = "Big Man" (king/ruler)
E.GAL *e-gal*	E (house) + GAL (big) = "Big House" (prison)

The above *Sumerian* examples begin with the 'standard' word or 'compound word' followed by a 'phonetic' and 'semantic' breakdown that leads us to the literal meaning. The illustrative point is that, for example, LUGAL is not translated with the subject first (as "Man-Big") but is "reversed" or translated "backwards" to denote a "King" by the literal phrase "big man." The subject is defined first (a 'man') and then the supportive (descriptive) element is added. In this example, the choice of the 'word' meaning *"big"* denotes social status and not a literally 'large' person in terms of size. To clarify the other examples provided, a KAMAH or "Great Gate" is generally the largest 'gate to the city'. First the "Gate" is identified as the subject. The same applies to E.GAL, although here we see more ancient 'word-play' still used today, for literally the *"big house"* (E.GAL) is the *Sumerian* word for "prison."

PHONICS – Syllables & Determinatives

As part of the *Akkadian* development of the *cuneiform* 'writing system', the original 'root-word' *ideography* became increasingly supplemented by 'syllabic' use of 'signs'. Far removed from the original 'pictorial' representations of literal objects and ideas, this new abstract innovation in writing allowed the 'signs' to also represent 'sounds'.

Languages that adopted the *cuneiform* writing system are considered '*agglutinative*', meaning that many of the 'complex' words are not really 'new' words, but large compound words that derive from one or more roots, coupled with whatever *affixes* and *determinative* are appropriate. This became increasingly simplified as the *cuneiform* writing system began to be looked at as a series of 'signs' based on phonetic 'syllables' as opposed to graphic representations of literal aspects.

While still considered *cuneiform*, the 'writing system' of the Akkadians (and later Assyrians) increasingly used 'signs' to represent possible 'syllables' or consonant-vowel combinations drawn from their own language. This means that in post-*Sumerian* writing, the 'signs' may be used to denote the original intended meaning (by the *Sumerians*) or another world altogether, with the 'sound' associated with the sound being implied regardless of the original 'graphic representation' and 'semantic meaning' of the 'sign'. Of course, different 'signs' can be used to denote the same (or a similar) syllable, just as a single 'sign' can be representative of different syllables! Learning these languages requires patience!

The concepts of 'prefixes' (before a word) and 'suffixes' (after a word) are certainly not 'foreign' to users of the English language. Such 'affixes' are typically added to a 'root' in order to denote additional 'context' to the 'word' given. *Cuneiform* has one unique addition to this, however, called the *determinative*.

A *determinative* is also a 'prefix' (or 'suffix') to a written word, but it may not always be spoken in 'vocalized' language speech. The more common *determinative* 'signs' are used separately than their original 'semantic meaning' or even 'phonetic' sound. They are used in the written word to 'distinguish' or 'determine' the nature of the 'subject' or 'object' being defined (or described).

A perfect 'determinative' example is the 'sign' for AN (or dingir). By itself, the sign might be used to refer to "heaven," "sky," "god" or even "star," but when used as a determinative prefix to a name, it denotes that name as a 'god'. For example, the word SAMAS could indicate either the literal "sun" or, if it is prefixed with AN (ilu or dingir), the Anunnaki deity (Samas) named for the "sun."

When dealing with the subject-nature of "divinity," transcribers have generally preferred to adopt the word 'dingir' for 'divine' or 'god' (as a determinative) and note it in their texts with a lower-case "d." Therefore, many transcriptions baring Anunnaki names, such as MARDUK or SAMAS, will usually render them as "d-MARDUK" and "d-SAMAS." [Cuneiform determinatives are often 'super-scripted' for transliterations using Latin letters so as to distinguish the characters/'signs' from the 'core' word.]

Another popular determinative used in Sumerian cuneiform is the prefix "ges-" or "gis-," meaning "wood." Whether attached to a type or species-name of a tree or something made of wood, the determinative "ges-" already informs the reader (interpreter) at the beginning of the word that we are dealing with something involving 'wood' or 'trees'.

For this application, one could note that the original 'sign' is indicative specifically and literally of 'wood', but its application as a determinative is extended to include all manner of trees and anything that is made from wood. This means that when inscribing (or translating) a 'sign' (or 'signs') to be read as "chair" or "board" or "handle" (etc.), the use of a determinative like "ges-" will automatically attribute the property of 'wooden' (or from a 'tree') to this word (even if it is not always incorporated into common 'vocalized' language (speech).

Refined uses of *cuneiform* are reflective of 'syllabic' syntax as opposed to direct/literal graphic represent-ation. 'Syllabic' uses of *cuneiform* often rely on the scribe to transform certain "words" into CV or VC[43] in order to be consistent in writing. Vowels can be shared in syllabic breakdowns. When two vowels must be next to each other, they are usually separated by an apostrophe. For example: BA'U (the female *Anunnaki* consort of NINURTA). To further illustrate C-V-C syllabic methods, the *Sumerian* word "HAD" (meaning 'bright' or 'shining') can be represented with a 'sign' to indicate "HAD" or it could be written phonetically as "HA-AD." There is a 'sign' for "MAH," or it could be written "MA-AH." And finally consider "DUGGA" as "DUG-GA" or "DU-UG-GA."

---

43 C-V-C Syllable Method – "CV" is consonant-vowel; "VC" is vowel-consonant.

THE CUNEIFORM EVOLUTION
(SUMERIAN → AKKADIAN)

"AB" – Sumerian Cuneiform (c. 3000-2500 B.C.)

"AB" – Akkadian-Babylonian (c. 2100 B.C.)

"EN" – Sumerian Cuneiform (c. 3000-2500 B.C.)

"EN" – Akkadian-Babylonian (2100 B.C.)

SEXAGESIMAL MATHEMATICS
OF MESOPOTAMIA

The traditional (classical) numeric system dominating the contemporary worldview is a *"base-10"* system; 'wholes' are considered 'multiples' of '10', particularly when a whole is multiplied by '10'. For example, '10' is considered a 'decade' and whole number with individual 'digits' are represented by ten unique symbols.[44]

Mathematical notation is not only a part of conscious understanding, both the characters and the 'name-title' designations for digits and operations are integral to a culture or language. 'Numeral Systems' are actually 'writing systems', or rather, considered to be a mutual (consistent) part of any specific writing system.[45]

The numeric system adopted in ancient Mesopotamia is known as *sexagesimal*, meaning: *"base-60."* Rather than '10' being the base (as is clearly seen in the modern 'metric' adoption of tens, hundreds, decades,

---

44 The modern 'numeric system' using the familiar shapes {seen here as: 1, 2, 3, 4, 5, 6, 7, 8, 9, 0} is a European development on the classical "Hindu-Arabic numeral system" originating in ancient India and is, itself, a progression of the "Brahmi numerals." The system was used first by Arabs and Persians before being introduced to Europe (c. 1000 AD).

45 Although from two different source origins, the European refinement of the "Hindu-Arabic numer-al system" was integrated as a standard with the (Roman) "*Latin*" alphabet. Combined they are considered part of the same (post-modern) standard 'writing system' adopted in the Western world.

centuries and percents), the *sexagesimal* system is based on 'sixty'.[46] The *sexagesimal* system was an integral part of the language, cultural economics and religious spirituality by the ancient *Sumerians* and *Babylonians*.

Sexagesimal 'base-60' mathematics is something best acquainted to our modern society in our perception of "time." Rather than the division of an hour into hundredths and percents, we can see an hour of 'sixty minutes' as the 'whole pie'. A 'quarter' of that 'pie', while still literally 25% (in 'base-10' terms), is not quantified by the value of '25', but is '15' (which is 25% of 60). With sixty seconds in a minute and sixty minutes in an hour, we can see clearly that "time" is still representative of *Sumerian* mathematics.[47]

The number '60' is considered the most 'sacred' numeric value in the *Sumerian* tradition. It has twelve factors[48] – '12' being the number representative of 'measu-

46 Some scholars have argued that 'Mesopotamian Mathematics' was not a true *sexagesimal 'base-60'* numeric system because they did not use sixty distinct 'numeric' symbols for digits. The modern system has ten, which can be repeated and grouped with place values to form other amounts.

47 Considerable portions of this chapter are based on the section titled "Mesopotamian Numerology" in Mardukite "*Liber-50*" released as "*Sumerian Religion*" by Joshua Free, which has been recently updated and revised in a new 2012 Second Edition (that also includes critical excerpts from "*Babylonian Myth & Magic*" {*Liber-51*} by Joshua Free) published as: "*Sumerian Religion: Secrets of the Anunnaki & The Origins of Babylon*."

48 Factors are the numeric values that can be multiplied to reach the desired among (60 in this example).

rement' in general as it applies to "time" and "space."[49]
Many simple fractions can be derived from the *sexages-imal* system using the factors to divide '60' into whole amounts. The factors are: 1, 2, 3, 4, 5, 6, 10, 12, 15, 20, 30, and of course, 60.[50]

Mathematical functions of 'addition', 'subtraction' and 'multiplication' were all observed similar to modern times. However, numbers were never divided and were instead reached by the 'multiplication of the recipro-cal'. For example, '60' is not "divided" by '10' to result in '6', instead, '60' is multiplied by 'one-tenth'.

The ancient *Sumerians* understood the connection bet-ween cycles, time and mathematics. In addition to the pragmatic use of the 'wheel' or 'circle' functionally, the *Sumerians* also were the first to develop the calculation that the circle was equivalent to 360 'degrees'.[51] This quantity was first based on a 'spiritual belief' and later became the basis of 'geometry' (literally "earth meas-uring"). Consequently, the "year"[52] was thought to pos-sess 360 days, being a complete '*earth cycle*'.

---

49 Note that there are '12 inches' in a standard 'foot'
   measurement and two sets of 12 hours dividing a single day
   (of 24 hours).
50 Sixty is the "lowest common multiple" shared by 1, 2, 3, 4,
   5 and 6. This means that sixty is the smallest value that is
   able to be evenly divided by every number from 1 to 6.
51 Statement excerpted from "*Babylonian Myth & Magic*"
   (*Liber-51*) as it appears in the newly revised and expanded
   Second Edition of "*Sumerian Religion: Secrets of the
   Anunnaki & The Origins of Babylon*" (*Liber-50*) by Joshua
   Free.
52 Annual Year = "*sat-ti*"

'6' x '1' x '60' = '360' { earth-time, local (earth) cycles }[53]

The *Sumerians* and *Babylonians* divided the cyclic year (360) into '12' periods (or divisions) of '30' days (or degrees). These periods were related to the 'moon' and called 'moonths', or more appropriately "months."

Originally, the 'annual' (cyclic) "year" was only divided into three seasons, essentially dubbed "beginning,"[54] "middle"[55] and "end."[56] Ancient 'sky-wise' *Babylonian* astronomers were aware of thirteen actual 'lunar' cycles in a solar "year," which caused them to include a shorter '13th month' into their calendars. Even by today's standards, the 'calender-year' requires "leap years" and does not account for the ever-changing position of 'celestial bodies' as they steadily move toward or away from one another.

𒁹	1	𒌋𒁹	11	𒎙𒁹	21	𒌍𒁹	31	𒐏𒁹	41	𒐐𒁹	51
𒈫	2	𒌋𒈫	12	𒎙𒈫	22	𒌍𒈫	32	𒐏𒈫	42	𒐐𒈫	52
𒐈	3	𒌋𒐈	13	𒎙𒐈	23	𒌍𒐈	33	𒐏𒐈	43	𒐐𒐈	53
𒐉	4	𒌋𒐉	14	𒎙𒐉	24	𒌍𒐉	34	𒐏𒐉	44	𒐐𒐉	54
𒐊	5	𒌋𒐊	15	𒎙𒐊	25	𒌍𒐊	35	𒐏𒐊	45	𒐐𒐊	55
𒐋	6	𒌋𒐋	16	𒎙𒐋	26	𒌍𒐋	36	𒐏𒐋	46	𒐐𒐋	56
𒐌	7	𒌋𒐌	17	𒎙𒐌	27	𒌍𒐌	37	𒐏𒐌	47	𒐐𒐌	57
𒐍	8	𒌋𒐍	18	𒎙𒐍	28	𒌍𒐍	38	𒐏𒐍	48	𒐐𒐍	58
𒐎	9	𒌋𒐎	19	𒎙𒐎	29	𒌍𒐎	39	𒐏𒐎	49	𒐐𒐎	59
𒌋	10	𒎙	20	𒌍	30	𒐏	40	𒐐	50		

---

53 As given in (*Liber-50*), released as "*Sumerian Religion*" by Joshua Free.

54 Beginning of Year = "*res sat-ti*"

55 Middle of Year = "*misil sat-ti*"

56 End of Year = "*kit sat-ti*"

Mesopotamian *sexagesimal* mathematics possesses a "sub-base" of '10'. The 'written symbols' originally used to represent 'numeric values' are 'hash-marks' and 'tallies'. In the *cuneiform* 'writing system', a simple 'wedge-mark' or 'sign' repeated in sets of ten. No "zero" exists within this system to either denote 'nothingness' or to hold the 'tens' place in a digit.[57]

A numeric (mathematical) system was adopted in ancient Mesopotamia as a means of quantifying (or measuring) the human experience of reality in worldly systems. The standard was developed initially as a means to facilitate (economic) commerce.

The *cuneiform* numeric designations (shown on page 56) are *Babylonian* (*Akkadian*) in origin, not necessarily *Sumerian* proper. The concept of 'abstract values' are not represented in the original 'Archaic' *Sumerian* system of *cuneiform* or the language. For example, the word for "cow" denotes "one cow," but there is no sp-

---

57 Mesopotamian mathematics did not include the value or symbol of *zero*. *Cuneiform* numerals were often separated by a blank space or a place holder (represented by a 'sign' of two small slanted wedges, the same sign used by the ancients as 'quotation marks'). This 'sign' was never used alone (never used to denote "zero" or nothing) or to represent tens places (never used at the end or right hand side of a number to denote 100's, 1000's, etc.). The idea and symbol for *zero* emerged from the later developed "Hindu-Arabic numeric system," from which the traditional (0 through 9) digits are derived for modern standardization. The number "zero" (denoting 'nothing') and the digit "zero" (which can be used to denote 'tens' places) are two different 'semantic meanings' although the symbolic (sign) representation is the same.

ecific word designated for "one." Ancient measurements and the 'units' of quantity are often defined as 'theoretical comparisons' to some other 'object' or 'standard'. For example, the '*gun*', as a weight-unit, is recorded as the equivalent to "the weight a laden donkey can carry," and so on.[58]

The original (*Sumerian*) *Anunnaki* numeric designations run in increments of five from '5' to '60', allowing "space" or "positions" for the "Olympian Twelve"[59] to be plotted. The "*Enlilite Sumerian*" 'Pantheon of Twelve' is composed of ANU (60) and ANTU (55), ENLIL (50) and NINLIL (45), ENKI (40) and NINKI[60] (35), NANNA (30)[61] and NINGAL (25), SHAMMASH[62] (20), INANNA[63] (15),

---

58 The '*gun*' or "load" is equivalent to 3600 '*gin*' or "shekel" – 30,000 grams (or approx. 67 pounds).

59 Olympian Twelve – An ancient archetypal model of 'divine pantheons' (pantheism) that is rooted in the proto-Sumerian (proto-*cuneiform*) age when the relationship and understanding between 'humans' and 'gods' was founded. The same basic 'formula' or 'pattern' of 'roles and positions' is found in other global cultural 'mythologies', particularly the classical "Greeks", from which the term "Olympian Twelve" has been derived.

60 NINKI – Whose name is also given in some texts as DAMKINA.

61 NANNA – As representative of the 'moon', from which we have our measured 'months', the designation for NANNA (also called SIN in *Akkadian*) is 30, representative of the 'month'.

62 SHAMMASH – Whose name is also known as SAMAS in *Akkadian*.

63 INANNA – Whose name is also known as ISHTAR in *Akkadian*, which is closely related to "*istar*" or "*istari*" (plural), an *Akkadian* word for "goddess" ("goddesses").

ISHKUR (10) and NINMAH[64] (5). This antiquated panth-eon displays a 'supernal trinity' along with represent-atives of the moon, sun and Venus.[65]

Alongside the *Akkadian* refinement of the *cuneiform* 'writing system', the 'numeric system' was standard-ized for the first time in Mesopotamia by the *Babylon-ians*.[66] The new 'official' mathematics allowed for a numeric standard to be applied to societal calculations in systems of agriculture (commerce) and architecture (construction).

MESOPOTAMIAN MEASUREMENTS: CRITICAL LENGTHS

UNIT	RATIO	REAL VALUE	SUMERIAN-AKKADIAN	
Grain	1/180	0.0025 meters	se	*uttatu*
Finger	1/30	0.015 meters	**su-si**	*ubanu*
Foot	2/3	0.333 meters	**su-du-a**	*sizu*
Cubit	1	0.497 meters	**kus**	*ammatu*
Step	2	1.000 meter	**giri**	*sepu*
Reed	6	3.000 meters	**gi**	*qanu*
Rod	12	6.000 meters	**nindan**	*nindanu*
Cord	120	60.00 meters	**ese**	*aslu*

---

64 NINMAH – Whose name is also given in some texts as NINHURSAG.

65 The 'Supernal Trinity' is composed of three divine couples, ANU and ANTU, ENLIL and NINLIL, and ENKI and NINKI; then, NANNA for moon, SHAMMASH for sun and INANNA for Venus.

66 According to tablet records, the mathematical system in Mesopotamia was standardized during the shift in "Ages" (when the "Enlilite Sumerian" 'Age of the Bull' gave way to the "Mardukite Baby-lonian" 'Age of the Ram') in c. 2160 BC under the direction of King Naram-Sin. Prior to this stand-ardization, as many as twelve different 'counting systems' had been used by *Sumerians*.

MESOPOTAMIAN MEASUREMENTS: CRITICAL DISTANCES

UNIT	RATIO	REAL VALUE	SUMERIAN-AKKADIAN	
Rod	1/60	6.000 meters	**nindan**	*nindanu*
Cord	1/6	60.00 meters	**ese**	*aslu*
Cable	1	360.0 meters	**us**	*us*
League	30	10800 meters	**da-na**	*beru*

MESOPOTAMIAN MEASUREMENTS: CRITICAL AREAS

UNIT	RATIO	REAL VALUE	SUMERIAN-AKKADIAN	
Shekel	1/60	1 sq. meter	**gin**	*siqlu*
Garden	1	36 sq. meters	**sar**	*musaru*
1/4-Field	5	900 sq. meters	**uzalak**	*?*
1/2-Field	10	1800 sq. m.	**upu**	*ubu*
Field	100	3600 sq. m.	**iku**	*iku*
Estate	1800	64800 sq. m.	**bur**	*buru*

MESOPOTAMIAN MEASUREMENTS: CRITICAL VOLUMES

UNIT	RATIO	REAL VALUE	SUMERIAN-AKKADIAN	
Shekel	1/60	?	**gin**	*siqlu*
Bowl	1	1 liter	**sila**	*qu*
Vessel	10	10 liters	**ban**	*sutu*
Bushel	60	60 liters	**bar-ri-ga**	*parsiktu*
Gur-Cube	300	300 liters	**gur**	*kurru*

MESOPOTAMIAN MEASUREMENTS: CRITICAL MASS

UNIT	RATIO	REAL VALUE	SUMERIAN-AKKADIAN	
Grain	1/180	0.05 grams	**se**	*uttatu*
Shekel	1	9 grams	**gin**	*siqlu*
Pound	60	497.7 grams	**ma-na**	*manu*
Load	3600	30000 grams	**gun**	*biltu*

DECIPHERING CUNEIFORM

An academic (scholarly) pursuit toward the '*transliteration*'[67] and '*translation*'[68] of excavated *cuneiform* 'tablets' has ensued for the past 150 years. Although it receives little public attention, it is one facet of archeology that is *still* developing and growing in human consciousness. It is *not* a 'dead science', but is instead, a constantly growing and evolving one – as should be evident from the pursuits of the modern *Mardukite Research Organization.*

Since the inception of the fields – '*Assyriology*'[69] or '*Su-*

---

67 *Transliteration* – the standardization of a literary work for interpretation (or translation) by first transforming the word 'signs' ('letters' or 'characters') from its native '*writing* system' into a modern one. For our purposes, it is the substitution of '*cuneiform* signs' with '*Latin*' letters, while still retaining the original language.

68 *Translation* – after being 'transliterated' into a standardized form (with '*Latin*' letters), the meaning of the word-text is then transferred from its native 'language' into a modern one. For our purposes, it is the word-substitution of *Sumerian* and *Babylo-Akkadian* 'semantics' with '*English*' ones. The success is determined by how closely the 'semantic-meaning' of the communicated message really is when the '*English*' version is compared to the original 'native' one.

69 The original name given to the study of systems in ancient Mesopotamia was "Assyriology," which is a complete misnomer, given that the 'catch-all' term is used to describe a considerable amount of non-*Assyrian* aspects. The *Assyrians* were one of the relatively more recent 'systems' to be installed in Babylon and are certainly not reflective of the whole. The term '*Sumerology*' applies better, but it still

merology' – many "standards" and "rules" have been implemented by scholars in an attempt to provide cohesive records – transliterations and translations – of the available 'literature' left to us from the ancient scribes.

Modern *cuneiform* translators have been forced to overcome many grammatical and intellectual challenges while uncovering the messages echoing from the myriad of foreign 'signs' drawn onto clay tablets. Fortunately, being rooted in an archetypal literary tradition, the ancient scribes have been kind enough to provide us with a series of *Sumerian* and *Akkadian* "lexicons"[70] to assist.

One of the first clerical challenges that an enthusiast or scholar is going to encounter – which has been described previously in our current volume – is the wide array of '*homonyms*' and '*synonyms*'[71] found in *cuneiform* texts

---

may not be appropriately suggestive. '*Assyriology*' earned its name as a result of an *Assyrian* library in Nineveh being the first major 'discovery' to launch the modern 'scientific' pursuit.

70 *Lexicon* – usually a 'book' that is "for and about words." A lexicon can include the word as it is written, as it is spoken, the 'sign' or 'characters' used to represent it, the same meaning as it applies to similar or related languages in addition to any other relative notes on its use, origins and relationship with other words.

71 *Homonyms* are words that are pronounced (spelled) the same although they have different meanings and are represented by different signs. For our purposes, this means that you can have multiple 'signs' that each represent the same spoken 'word', each with a different semantic. *Synonyms* are words that are the same or have the same meaning although they are spelled and spoken entirely

from both the *Sumerians* and *Akkadians*.

To overcome some of the 'language' "issues', a system of 'numeric subscripts' and '*diacritics*'[72] was invented for modern purposes wherever 'transliteration' or 'translations' might be "left up to chance" by an interpreter. These are 'modern' functions meant for scholarly 'cohesion' purposes that are not critical for our purposes and therefore do not appear within our word catalogue.[73] Although not currently used by the *Mardukites*, the 'numeric subscript' (attached to vowels) is replacing the older '*diacritic*' notation among academicians to distinguish similarly spelled words.

As a standard, *Sumerian* words have traditionally been transliterated into 'lower-case' "*Latin*" (Romantic) letters. They appear in this manner for our own catalogues and we further distinguish them from surrounding text by using a '**bold**' face. Some standards dictate the use of 'lower-case' if-and-only-if the *Sumerian* is being isolated from other language use, otherwise it is displayed in 'CAPITAL' letters. This was found to be visually unappealing for our purposes.

Similar to *Sumerian* transliterations, the standard for *Akkadian* is that is should appear in 'lower-case' "*Latin*" (Romantic) letters as well, but '*italicized*'. The distinct-

---

differently and represented by different 'signs'.

72 The marks added to 'standardized letters' to denote 'inflection' and 'pronunciation'.

73 Making note of the "Tablet-I" work-list first appearing in *Liber-9* in 2009 (and reprinted in the complete Year-1 anthology "*Necronomicon Anunnaki Bible*") which was expanded upon for '*Liber-I*' ("*Secrets of Sumerian Language*") of which the current pocket handbook is excerpted from.

ion between the two is satisfyingly earned by using **'bold'** (*Sumerian*) and *'italics'* (*Akkadian*).

The presence of a transliterated word in 'CAPITALS' is best reserved for when such words make an appearance in the midst of other "*Latin*" letter writing.[74] Another common practice is to use 'CAPITALS' for the transliteration of "proper names," or at the very least, "deity names."

In some transliterations, it is not uncommon to find individual parts of a compound word separated by 'periods' between 'CAPITAL' letters. In our current work this only occurs to illustrate the parts of a compound word-name adopted by a deity. The breakdown of other compound words are illustrated in this text using 'hyphens' between 'lower case' letters.

Determinative 'signs' appear no different than they would otherwise. These *'affixes'* are used to denote the 'type' or 'category' that the main root (or 'stem') word is being used for. In modern transliterations *'determinatives'* are always given in 'super-scripted' 'lower-case' letters.[75] Most *'determinatives'* are used *before* a 'root-stem', though some appear *after*.

---

74 For example, if specific transliterated *Sumerian* or *Akkadian* words were being discussed in these otherwise 'English' paragraphs, it would be considered a 'nicety' on the part of the transcriber to set that word apart from the 'English' by introducing it in 'CAPITAL' letters.

75 This method is not used in the Mardukite work where no 'metascript' (either 'super-' or 'sub-') is actually employed. If necessary, the 'determinative' can be applied to a transliterated *Sumerian* word by *'italicizing'* it, and the opposite for *Akkadian*.

A few common *pre-determinatives*[76] in the *Sumerian* language are:

- **dingir**– (abbreviated as **d**–) : using the sign for *god*; the names of deities can be distinguished.
- **gis**– (or **ges**–) : using the sign for *tree*; the names of trees, types of wood and wooden objects can be distinguished.
- **kus**– : using the sign for *skin* the names of hides and other leather objects can be distinguished.
- **mul**– : using the sign for *stars* the names of constellations, stars and planets can be distinguished.

Whenever the reader-seeker is involved with the literal interpretation of the *cuneiform* 'writing system', whether *Sumerian*, *Akkadian*, or by some other tongue, it is important to remember that a single 'sign' can represent one or more 'logographic' values. A single word may be composed of several 'signs' and some of them may be 'determinatives' or have 'syllabic' purpose.

To perfectly master the *Sumerian* or *Akkadian* languages, or else the ancient use of *cuneiform* script in general, the reader-seeker would have to be expertly exponent in 'grammar' and 'linguistics'. This is primarily due to the myriad of basic 'rules' that apply to any language – even English (although they are generally taken for granted once one is socialized into their native tongue).

---

76 *Pre-determinatives* – 'determinatives' that appear *before* the root-stem 'word'.

Rather than create a text that would be grueling to use by anyone not already attending a university for 'graduate-level' scholar-ship in these pursuits, the purpose of the current volume is to bring the vocabulary and application of ancient *cuneiform* writing to its most accessible point for the 'common man'. As such, we are greatly simplifying matters in this chapter toward this.

In addition to the 'keys', 'rules', and 'standards' already addressed in our previous text, it is important to note that the *Sumerian* language does not offer us two critical written 'articles' – "*the*" and "*a.*" This means that a 'sign' representing a *'noun'*, for exam-ple, the 'sign' for "tree," can be read or used to denote "*a tree*," "*the* tree" or simply "tree." However, '*possessive suffixes*' can be added to a word. Transliterators distinguish them as separate from the 'root-stem' that they alter by hyphenating them.

The most common '*possessive suffixes*' include:

–gu	"*my*" or "*by my*"	and (**–ga**) "*in my*"
–zu	"*your*" or "*by your*"	and (**–za**) "*in your*"
–me	"*our*" or "*by our*"	and (**–me-a**) "*in our*"
–bi	"*its*"	and (**–be**) "*by its*"
		and (**–ba**) "*in its*"

The phrase "*my king*" versus "*your king*" is written:

lu-gal-gu (*lugalgu*) versus **lu-gal-zu** (*lugalzu*)

'*Performative prefixes*' can be added to the beginning of a word to indicate the "expressive action" of a term or subject. In the later *Akkadian* language, we see an increased use of proper "conjunctions" that replace some of the original *Sumerian* grammar. The most common *Sumerian* language '*performative prefixes*' include:

ba-ra-	*"can not . . ." / "must not . . ."*
ga- (gi–, gu–)	*"may I . . ." / "I shall . . ."*
he- (ha–, hu–)	*"may he . . ." / "he should . . ."*
na–	*"may he not . . ."*
na–	*"he shall . . ." / "shall he not . . ?"*
n-ga- (in-ga-)	*"and . . ." / "also . . ."*
nu- (la–, li–)	*"not . . ."*
nu-us–	*"if only . . ."*
si- (sa–, su–)	*"so . . ." / "therefore . . ."*
u- (a–, i–)	*"when . . ." / "after . . ."*

The following brief-concise mini-lexicon is provided as only an introduction to the actual language and use of *cuneiform* by the ancient *Sumerians* and *Akkadians*. It has been included to assist in familiarizing the seeker with further elements of *cuneiform* usage. A general 'theme' or 'concept' appears bold, capitalized and underlined to start the entry. The first two lines indicate the actual transcribed 'words' applicable; with *Sumerian* appearing first (in bold) under 'A', followed by the *Babylo*-Akkadian (in italics). The semantic or phonetic breakdown of the words (and other related terms from the respective language) immediately follow, with *Sumerian* (still bolded) listed with 'a' and the *Babylo-Akkadian* listed with 'b'. The large 'sign' that accompanies the entries is the best *cuneiform* representation of the key idea heading each section, using the *Sumerian* language as a baseline. The smaller uniform 'sign' that supplements it (when applicable) is derived from *Akkadian*. There are usually more 'words' and 'examples' provided in each section than are represented proper by the *cuneiform* example given.

SUMERIAN LANGUAGE

A.) **EMEGIR**
B.) *sumeritum, sumeru*
a.) 1. **eme-gir** : **eme** ('tongue') + **gir** ('native', 'local')
b.) 1. *sumeritum* ('a Sumerian'), 2. *sumeru* ('Sumerian')
3. *lisanu* ('tongue', 'language', 'speech')
4. *lisanum* (the 'native language' of anyone)
5. *lisanum sakiltu* ('native language of a foreigner')

NOTES: The word "*Sumerian*" is actually *Akkadian* in origin. It does not pertain to a 'location' as much as it does a 'language'. The ancient word for 'language' is "tongue." Being the first written language, the ancient *Sumerians* simply referred to their own as a "native tongue" (**emegir**). The 'signs' and words used to represent the concept of "tongue" can be used to denote 'language' or the literal part of the body ('tongue'). To differentiate themselves culturally and linguistically from their predecessors, the *Akkadians* used the regional location (inhabited lands) of the *Sumerians* to define them as a people and language. The *Akkadian* cuneiform 'sign' offered is for the word *lisanum*.

HEAVENS / SKY

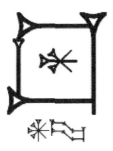

A.)   **AN, ANSAR, ZIKUM**

B.)   *samu, same*

a.)   1. **an** ('sky' or 'heaven') { see also: <u>GOD</u> }

         2. **an-sar** : **an** ('heavens') + **sar** ('area' or 'entirety')

         3. **an-zag** : **an** ('heaven') + **zag** ('border') = "horizon"

         4. **an-ur** : "house of Anu" or "horizon" (also **zikum**)

b.)   1. *sam-u, siamu* ('red-brown colored planet') = "heaven"

         2. *sama, samu* ('sky' or 'heaven') { see also: <u>GOD</u> }

         3. *same* ('heavens' or 'celestial'); plural form of *samu*

         4. *isid same* : *isid* ('base') + *same* ('heavens') = "horizon"

         5. *serret same* ('galaxy') { "the Milky Way" }

         6. *elat same* : *elat* ('heights') + *same* ('heavens') = "zenith"

         7. *simmilat same* ('stairway to heaven' or 'ladder to heaven')

<u>NOTES:</u> The traditional *cuneiform* sign for 'heaven', 'sky', 'god', 'star' and 'ANU' are based on the *Sumerian* AN (see the section on GOD). Here we see the zone or place of 'heaven' being designated as the 'house' or 'domain' of the chief *Anunnaki* deity, ANU.

GOD / GODDESS

A.)   **AN, DIGIR, DINGIR, ILU, ILUNI**

B.)   *an, ilu, iltu, istari, ilani*

a.)   1. **di(n)-gir** : **di(n)** ('judgment') + **gir** (decision/to deliver)

       1. **dingir** : "who decide/deliver the judgment"

       2. **an** : meaning 'heaven', 'star' or 'deity' in *Sumerian.*

       3. **ilu** : singular/All/One   4. **ilu-ni** : plural

b.)   1. *ilu* : ('god'; masc.)   2. *iltu* : ('goddess'; fem.)

       3. *ilutu* : *ilu* ('god') + *tu* ('life') = "life being as a god"

       3. *ilutu* : ('divinity' or 'deity'); literally : 'god'+'life'

       4. *ilani* : ('gods'; pl.)   5. *istari/istaru* : ('goddess')

       6. *ilumma* : "by god", "by the gods"   7. *ili* : "godly"

       8. *illil* : *il(u)+il(u)* = 'god of gods'; usually reserved for ENLIL

<u>NOTES:</u> The original *Sumerian* 'sign' is a **star**; four bars, eight pointed, from which the '*asterisk*' [*] (*Gr.* "little star") is derived. It is simplified in *Akkadian* as a **cross**; two bars, four points. As a determinative, the dingir/ilu 'sign' is placed before the name of a deity. Example: *ilu-MARDUK* or *d-MARDUK* is 'the god Marduk'.

DESTINY / FATE

A.) **NAM, NAMTAR**
B.) *namtaru, simtu*
a.) 1. **nam-tar** : **nam** ('fate') + **tar** ('to cut') = "to decree
    fate"
    1. **nam-tar** : "destiny"   2. **nam** : "fate"
    3. **dub-nam-tar-mes** ('Tablet of Destiny')
b.) 1. *namtaru* : "fate"   2. *simta-samu* = "to decree
    fate"
    3. *simtu* : "destiny" (what is 'fixed', 'established')
    4. *ina-simtu* : "inevitable", "inevitability",
       "necessary"
    5. *tupsimatu* : *tuppu* ('tablet') + *simati* = "Tablet of
       Destiny"

NOTES: Mesopotamian languages semantically differentiate between 'destiny' and 'fate'. "Fate" is one's 'lot' in life. It is when this has been 'fixed' or 'decreed' (presumably by the 'gods') that it becomes one's 'destiny'. This is referred to as the "Tablet of Destiny" – where an individual's 'life-program' is 'written'. The *Sumerian* word **namtar** was also used to denote 'disease', which was thought to come to one by way of a 'demon' or spiritual entity, or as a result of one's 'fate'.

**MARDUKITE
CHAMBERLAINS**

Would you like to know more???

ENTER THE REALM
OF THE

MARDUKITE
CHAMBERLAINS

NECRONOMICON ANUNNAKI BIBLE

Edited by Joshua Free

The Necronomicon – a masterpiece of Mesopotamian Magick, Mysticism and primordial spirituality!

A Complete Necronomicon!

This definitive edition contains the complete Year 1 tablet cycle from the "Mardukite Chamberlains" including Liber N – *Necronomicon*, Liber LL – *Liturgy & Lore*, Liber GG – *Gatekeepers Grimoire* and the coveted Liber 9. These are the raw underground materials have shaped the existence of man's beliefs and practices for thousands of years – right from the heart of Sumer, Babylon and Egypt! A Mardukite compendium of intensive historical, spiritual and mystical research drawn from very real and researchable tablets... enough to support a very real "*Necronomicon*" Anunnaki revival tradition!

Join hundreds of others who have enjoyed the best of what the next generation has to offer. What has come before is but a shadow to the realizations now capable to all self-honest Truth Seekers! Rediscover the most ancient records of magick and mysticism – the most ancient traditions of Gods and Men lay here waiting to be unveiled!

MARDUKITE

SUMERIAN RELIGION
by Joshua Free

The most highly acclaimed materials from the Mardukites: an account of the evolution of the Sumerian Tradition into Babylonian (and beyond) such as the modern world has never before had access to.

Developed by the next generation of seekers actively using this revival tradition in present day – not merely the presentation of dry academic renderings of obscure tablets: *Sumerian Religion* will take you on a progressive journey that is just as relevant and critical today as it was thousands of years ago – *if not more so.*

Sumerian Religion is the perfect practical companion to *all systems and traditions* as it displays the origins of human traditions on the planet, something which all can relate to. As unique as it is practical – supporting a revival tradition revealing the nature, origins and traditions connected to the "Star-Gates" of the *Anunnaki Alien Gods of Mesopotamia*, which the public contemporary society has previously only known through nearly insubstantial renderings. A clearly understood volume offering a revolutionary perspective towards understand-ing Life, the Universe & Everything!

GATES OF THE NECRONOMICON

Edited by Joshua Free

The complete Year 2 Liber 50+51+R anthology of the Mardukites with "Sumerian Religion", "Babylonian Myth & Magic" and "Necronomicon Revelations."

"Sumerian Religion" (Liber 50) will take you on a unique progressive journey that is just as relevant and critical today as it was thousands of years ago.

"Babylonian Myth & Magic" (Liber 51) is unparalleled in displaying the post-Sumerian mystery tradition of the ancient Babylonians. Discover how Babylon rose to the heights of its power from seemingly prehistoric nothingness and how these systems are still with us!

"Necronomicon Revelations" (Liber R) illustrates how spiritual beings have influenced the imaginations of 'metaphysical' artists and writers, increasingly during the last century. Discover the forces that are behind all of the systems installed in human consciousness, both 'social' and 'mystical', since the time of the ancient Sumerian Anunnaki.

SECRETS OF SUMERIAN LANGUAGE
by Joshua Free

The concise, practical and economical guide to cuneiform writing systems – released from the Mardukite vaults for the first time!

Discover the secret origins and use of societal language, psychological (and spiritual) impact corresponding with the inception and control of human systems and how to analyze and interpret cuneiform logograms "signs", semantics and phonetics utilized for both Sumerian and Akkadian (Babylonian) tablet writings.

Ever popular in the underground, this book simplifies the scribe's art of tablet transliteration and translation by providing clear definition to thousands of words, over 500 illustrated easy-to-read cuneiform signs and comparative cross-reference tables for Sumerian, Akkadian (Babylonian) and English semantics!

Edition Note: "*Secrets of Sumerian Language*" represents the complete "*Liber-I*" volume of which the current pocket handbook ("*The Truth Seeker's Guide to Cuneiform*") has been excerpted.

THE BOOK OF MARDUK
by Joshua Free

The original Anunnaki devotional companion of the modern revival returns in an oversized full-color deluxe ceremonial edition!

The Book of Marduk (by Nabu) is a long-lost out-of-print 'tablet collection' that paved the way for intensive research and experimentation using Joshua Free's 'Necronomicon Anunnaki Bible' and essentially comprises the internal methods of the 'Order of Nabu' to acquire communication and establish a relationship with 'alien intelligences' via a program of ancient-styled Babylonian-inspired 'Mardukite' initiation, dedication and devotion; reviving the same process used by ancient priests of the Sumerian Anunnaki in Mesopotamia.

Original never-before-seen 'incantation-prayers' appear in both English and Akkadian/Babylonian.

The 'Book of Marduk' composes *Liber-W* and the Tablet-W series of the revised and expanded fifth edition of the 'Necronomicon Anunnaki Bible' edited by Joshua Free.

ABOUT THE AUTHOR
JOSHUA FREE

Known as "Merlyn Stone" in the 1990's, **Joshua Free** reappeared on the scene in 2008 with the launch of *Mardukite Ministries* on the Summer Solstice that year.

He is the *Archbishop-Patesi* of the *Mardukite Archdiocese of North America* and the *Mardukite Chamberlains, Nabu Maerdechai*. Joshua is also the founder of the *NexGen Systemology Society*.

His prolific writings include: *Arcanum, Book of Elven-Faerie, Sumerian Religion, Necronomicon Anunnaki Bible,* and *The Sorcerer's Handbook of Merlyn Stone* among several others.

In 2011 he released his first published work of fiction titled *The Hybrids*.

Printed in Great Britain
by Amazon